# Th...
# THE BEST
# OF THE ELEPHANT
# JOKE BOOK

### belongs to

_____

CW00847843

Also available in Beaver by Katie Wales

**THE ELEPHANT JOKE BOOK**
**JOKES FROM OUTER SPACE**
**SANTA'S CHRISTMAS JOKE BOOK**

# THE RETURN OF THE ELEPHANT JOKE BOOK

## Katie Wales

### Illustrated by Mark Burgess

**Beaver Books**

A Beaver Book
Published by Arrow Books Limited
62-65 Chandos Place, London WC2N 4NW

An imprint of Century Hutchinson Limited

London Melbourne Sydney Auckland
Johannesburg and agencies throughout the world

First published 1988
Reprinted 1988 and 1989

Text © Katie Wales 1988
Illustrations © Century Hutchinson Ltd 1988

This book is sold subject to the condition that
it shall not, by way of trade or otherwise, be lent,
resold, hired out, or otherwise circulated without
the publisher's prior consent in any form of
binding or cover other than that in which it is
published and without a similar condition
including this condition being imposed on the
subsequent purchaser.

Set in Century Schoolbook
by JH Graphics Ltd, Reading

Made and printed in Great Britain
by Courier International Ltd, Tiptree, Essex

ISBN 0 09 959420 X

*To: John Walter Ainsworth, Saqar Aljafari, Lindsey Allerton, Tracey Andrews, Tia Banerjee, Emma Bradley, Emma Louise Breeze, Mark Cieslik, Marie Cowgill, Robin and Jenny Derwent, Eleanor Dobing, Christopher Durman, John Easton, Juliet Field, Gareth Foster, Helen Fox, Thomas and William Gibson, Faye Hamlet, Mandy Hill, Amy Holliman, Rebecca Jackson, Sarah Kendall, David Kent, Roy Ledingham, James Martindale, Catherine Marsden, Sabina Mapley, Graham Paddick, Katie Poole, W. M. Rigg, Lucy Roberts, Charlotte Louisa Rose, Craig Rutherford, Lyn Rutherford, Rebecca Sanders, the Sawyers, Polyanne Jolie Shaw, Tim Wales, Sarah Ward; also Angela from Rochford, Lindsay from Bewdley, and Rachel from Walton, Somerset.*

# Contents

What is . . .                          9
What do you get if . . .          ·    24
What . . .                            34
What do you call . . .                43
What's the difference . . .           46
Why . . .                             49
How . . .                             60
Who, Which, Where . . .               66
Did you hear . . .                    70
Jumbo talk . . .                      74
Jumbo jingles . . .                   77
Tail-pieces . . .                     78

# What is . . .

What is grey on the inside and yellow on the
outside?
*An elephant disguised as a banana.*

What is big and grey with red spots?
*An elephant with measles.*

What is big and grey and always points north?
*A magnetic elephant.*

What is big and grey and needs no ironing?
*A drip-dry elephant.*

What is big and grey and goes slam, slam?
*A two-door elephant.*

What is big and grey and soapy, and goes
round and round?
*An elephant in a washing machine.*

What is the first thing an elephant does in the
morning?
*Gets up.*

**What is big and grey and good at sums?**
*An elephant with a pocket calculator.*

**What is big and grey and bounces?**
*An elephant on a pogo stick.*

**What is big and red and has a trunk?**
*An elephant holding its breath.*

What is big and grey, has a trunk and climbs trees?
*An elephant — I lied about it climbing trees.*

What is the best thing to do if a rampaging elephant breaks your front door down?
*Run out of the back door.*

What is big and grey and red all over?
*An elephant with nappy rash.*

What else?
*A sunburnt elephant.*

What else?
*An elephant embarrassed by all these elephant jokes.*

What is big and grey and wears a mask?
*The Lone Elephant.*

What is worse than an elephant with hay fever?
*A centipede with fallen arches.*

What is an elephant after it is 6 months old?
*7 months old.*

What is grey, has a trunk and jumps every
3 minutes?
*An elephant with hiccups.*

What is big and grey and has 2 trunks?
*An elephant going on holiday.*

What is green and has a trunk?
*A seasick tourist.*

What is big and grey and has 16 wheels?
*An elephant on roller skates.*

13

**What is grey and has big ears and 2 wheels?**
*An elephant on a motorbike.*

**What is brown and has 4 legs and a trunk?**
*A mouse coming back from its holiday.*

**What is big, grey and blue and is found at the North Pole?**
*A lost elephant.*

**What is big and grey and goes crunch, crunch?**
*An elephant eating potato crisps.*

What is big and grey and hides in the wardrobe?
*An elephant that owes money.*

What else?
*An elephant afraid of the thunder.*

What is worse than an elephant on water skis?
*A porcupine in a rubber ring.*

What is black and weighs 2 tons?
*A chocolate-covered elephant.*

What is big and grey and covered in fur?
*An elephant in a mink coat.*

What is grey and powdery?
*Instant elephant.*

What is the best way to catch an elephant?
*Act like a nut and he'll follow you anywhere.*

What is grey, then yellow, then grey, then yellow?
*An elephant rolling down a hill with a buttercup in its trunk.*

What is big and grey and goes round and round?
*An elephant stuck in a revolving door.*

What is an elephant's favourite instrument?
*A trumpet.*

What is big, grey and beautiful and wears glass slippers?
*Cinderellaphant.*

**What is an elephant's least favourite instrument?**
*A piano.*


**What is big and grey and sings jazz?**
*Ellaphants Gerald.*


**What is big, red and white, and hates to be touched?**
*A sunburnt elephant.*


**What is grey, has 2 wings and gives money to baby elephants?**
*The tusk fairy.*

What is big and grey and weighs 4 tons?
*A mouse built to government specifications.*

What is the hardest thing about learning to ride an elephant?
*The ground!*

What is big and blue, has a trunk and can't climb trees?
*A blue denim elephant.*

What is the best way to tell a circus elephant with a bad temper that he's fired?
*Call him long distance.*

What is grey, has 4 door and goes beep, beep, beeeeeeep?
*A 4-door elephant with a jammed horn.*

What is big and grey and coughs?
*An elephant with a bad chest.*

What is big and grey and goes clump, clump, swish, swish?
*An elephant with flippers on his back feet.*

What is big and grey and flies?
*An elephant in a helicopter.*

What else?
*A jumbo jet.*

What is big and grey one minute and turns white the next?
*An elephant in a microwave oven.*

What is big and grey one minute and turns white the next?
*An elephant in a deep freeze.*

What is the elephants' favourite football team?
*Trunkmere Rovers.*

What is grey then brown, grey then brown,
grey then brown?
*An elephant on a barbecue spit.*

What is the elephant's least favourite carol?
*'The Holly and the Ivory'.*

What is feathered and crossed the Alps with
elephants?
*Hennibal's Army.*

What is big and grey and counts
to 10 backwards?
*An elephant with hiccups.*

What is the elephants' favourite Underground
station?
*The Elephant and Castle.*

What is big and grey and goes bleep, bleep?
*An elephone.*

What else?
*A telephant.*

What is big and grey and lives in a Scottish lake?
*Nessie the Elephant.*

What is big and grey and makes a horrible noise?
*An elephant playing the bagpipes.*

What is white on the outside, grey on the
inside and lays heavy on your stomach?
*An elephant sandwich.*

What is big and grey and goes up and
down 20 times a day?
*An elephant doing press-ups.*

What is 2 feet long, has 32 eyes and 2 tongues?
*An elephant's sneakers.*

What is big and grey and would kill you if it
fell out of a tree?
*An elephant.*

**What is big and yellow and has a blocked trunk?**
*An elephant drowning in a bowl of custard.*

**What is big and grey and protects you from the rain?**
*An umbrellaphant.*

**What is big and grey and plays squash?**
*An elephant in a cupboard.*

# What do you get if . . .

What do you get if you cross an elephant with a penguin?
*Big flippers.*

What do you get if you cross an elephant with a ghost?
*A big nothing.*

What do you get if you cross an elephant with a budgie?
*A messy cage.*

What do you get if you cross a ballpoint pen
with an elephant?
*The Ink-credible Hulk.*

What do you get if you cross an elephant with a
rabbit?
*I don't know, but there would be lots of them in
a very short time.*

What do you get if you cross an elephant with a
light bulb?
*A huge electricity bill.*

What do you get if you cross an elephant with a
sheep?
*Enough wool to knit a skyscraper.*

What do you get if you cross an elephant with a
swarm of locusts?
*I'm not sure, but watch out!*

What do you get if you cross an elephant with a
spider?
*I don't know, but if it crawls across the ceiling,
it will collapse.*

What do you get if you cross an elephant with a
goose?
*An animal that honks before it runs you over.*

What do you get if you cross an elephant with a woodpecker?
*An animal that knocks before it runs you over.*

What do you get if you cross an elephant with an insect?
*A forget-me-gnat.*

What do you get if you cross an elephant with a monkey?
*A swinging elephant.*

What do you get if you cross a zebra with an elephant?
*A traffic jam.*

What do you get if you cross a cow with an elephant?
*Long-life milk.*

What do you get if you cross an elephant with a canary?
*I don't know, but when it sings, it makes a terrible noise!*

What do you get if you cross an elephant with a cactus?
*The biggest porcupine in the world.*

What do you get if you cross an elephant with a cockerel?
*An animal that wakes people living in the next town.*

What do you get if you cross an elephant with a caretaker?
*A 2-ton corridor sweeper.*

What do you get if you cross an elephant with a jar of jam?
*Jam sandwiches that never forget.*

What do you get if you cross an elephant with a lump of dough?
*A giant meat loaf.*

What do you get if you cross an elephant with a pigeon?
*A big mess.*

What do you get if you cross an elephant with a cat?
*Very scared mice.*

What else?
*An animal that puts YOU out at night!*

What do you get if you cross an elephant with a mouse?
*Very scared cats.*

What do you get if you cross an elephant with a porcupine?
*An extra large brush.*

What do you get if you cross an elephant with an orange?
*Orange squash.*

What do you get if you cross an elephant with an apple?
*A stomach ache.*

What do you get if you cross an elephant with a potato field?
*Mashed potatoes.*

What do you get if you cross an elephant with a squirrel?
*An animal that remembers where it hid its nuts.*

**What do you get if you cross an elephant with a dog?**
*An animal that remembers where it buried its bones.*

**What do you get if you cross an elephant with a kangaroo?**
*Flat Australians.*

**What do you get if you cross an elephant with a bat?**
*Collapsed belfries.*

**What do you get if you cross an elephant with Dracula?**
*An animal that sucks your blood through its trunk.*

What do you get if you cross an elephant with a vacuum cleaner?
*A Hoover that sucks only peanuts.*


What do you get if you cross an elephant with a gooseberry?
*A pie that never forgets.*


What do you get if you cross an elephant with a bee?
*Squashed flowers.*

What do you get if you cross an elephant with
an ant?
*Anthills as big as Mount Everest.*

What do you get if you cross an elephant with a
chicken?
*Enough feathers to fill a duvet.*

What else?
*Scrambled eggs.*

What do you get if you cross the Underground
with an elephant?
*Blocked Tubes.*

What do you get if you cross an elephant with a
rubber band?
*An animal that never forgets snap decisions.*

What do you get if you cross an elephant with a
banana?
*I don't know, but I wouldn't try peeling it!*

What do you get if you cross an elephant
with 2 banana skins?
*A pair of slippers.*

What do you get if you cross a river with an elephant?
*To the other side.*

What do you get if you cross an elephant with a skunk?
*A big stinker.*

What do you get if you cross the Alps with an elephant?
*A sore bottom!*

# What . . .

**What makes more noise than an angry elephant?**
*2 angry elephants.*

**What do elephants sing at Christmas?**
*'Jungle bells, jungle bells.'*

What did the dog say to the elephant?
*'Woof, woof.'*

What goes 'Ha, ha,' bonk?
*An elephant laughing his head off.*

If storks bring human babies, what bring baby
elephants?
*Cranes.*

What else?
*Storks with hernias.*

What goes out grey and comes in white?
*An elephant in a snow storm.*

If an elephant crosses the road, rolls in the
mud and crosses back again, what is it?
*A dirty double-crosser.*

What do you find between an elephant's toes?
*Slow-moving pygmies.*

**What weighs 2 tons, is grey and loves pizza?**
*An Italian elephant.*

**What weighs 2 tons, is grey and loves curry?**
*An Indian elephant.*

**What weighs 2 tons, is grey and loves fish and chips?**
*An English elephant.*

**What weighs 2 tons and is covered with lettuce and relish?**
*A Big Mac-elephant.*

**What happens to old elephant jokes?**
*They fall flat.*


**What did Thomas Edison Elephant invent?**
*The electric peanut.*


**What did Mrs Elephant say to Mr Elephant?**
*'I hear the thunder of tiny feet.'*


**What side of an elephant has most skin?**
*The outside.*


**What happened when the elephant sat on Katie Wales's sofa?**
*She had to go and buy a new one.*

If an elephant always remembers, what animal always forgets?
*An owl; it's always saying, 'Who? who?'*


What does NUDE mean?
*National Union of Dim Elephants.*


What goes bumpety-bump, bumpety-bump?
*An elephant falling down the stairs.*


What do you do with a green elephant?
*Wait till it ripens.*


What do you do if an elephant sneezes?
*Get out of the way.*


What have Rupert the Bear and Nellie the Elephant in common?
*Their middle name.*


What happened to the canoe when the elephant got in it?
*It sank.*

**What looks like an elephant and flies?**
*A flying elephant.*

What do elephants say when they bump into each other?
*'Small world, isn't it!'*

What did the elephant say when the tiger grabbed his tail?
*'That's the end of me.'*

What did the elephant say when it was bitten by a snake?
*Nothing: elephants can't talk.*

What weighs a ton, has 4 legs and talks?
*Two half-ton parrots.*

What goes in grey and comes out blue?
*An elephant swimming on a cold day.*

What did the grey elephant say to the blue elephant?
*'Cheer up!'*

What was the elephant doing on the M1?
*About 1 mile per hour.*


What did the cobbler say when a herd of
elephants came into his shop?
*'Shoe!'*


What has 2 heads, 6 feet, 1 tail, 4 ears and a
trunk?
*A man riding an elephant.*

**What goes trump, trump, SPLAT?**
*An elephant tripping over a bowl of custard.*

**What goes trump, trump, 'EEK!'**
*An elephant that's just seen a mouse.*

**What goes trump, trump, SQUASH?**
*An elephant crossing the M25.*

**What goes trump, trump, BANG?**
*An elephant in a minefield.*

**What goes trump, trump, BOOM?**
*An elephant falling over a cliff.*

What happened when the circus elephant
tripped up?
*He pulled out the tails of 6 elephants in front.*

What weighs a ton, is bald and sucks lollipops?
*Elly Savalas.*

What did the zoo keeper see when an elephant
squirted water from its trunk?
*A jumbo jet.*

What does an elephant do if he breaks his toe?
*Gives up ballet dancing.*

# What do you call . . .

What do you call people who like elephants?
*Ele-fans.*

What do you call an ant with big ears?
*An eleph-ant.*

What do you call an elephant with a banana in each ear?
*Anything, it can't hear you.*

What do you call a man who's eaten an elephant?
*Full up.*

What do you call a Jumbo with a machine gun?
*Jambo.*

What do you call a metre-high elephant?
*Trunkated.*

What do you call an elephant in rubber boots?
*A welly-phant.*

What do you call a fat elephant who drowns in a river?
*A non-slimmer.*

What do you call an elephant hitch-hiker?
*A 2-ton pick up.*

What do you call an elephant with a hand grenade?
*Sir!*

What do you call a female elephant
with 6 children?
*Mum.*

**What did Wally call his pet elephant?**
*Rover.*

**What do you call an elephant witch doctor?**
*Mumbo Jumbo.*

**What does an Indian elephant call an African elephant?**
*Big Ears.*

**What do you call an elephant in a fridge?**
*A tight squeeze.*

**What do you call an Irish elephant?**
*Kelly-phant.*

**What do you call an elephant hitch-hiker?**
*Stranded.*

# What's the difference . . .

What's the difference between an elephant and
a grapefruit?
*An elephant is grey.*

What's the difference between an elephant
with tusk-ache and a rainstorm?
*One roars with pain and the other pours with
rain.*

What's the difference between an elephant and
a gooseberry?
*Elephants don't grow on bushes.*

What's the difference between an elephant and
a ginger nut?
*Dip it in your tea, and if it goes soggy, it's a
ginger nut.*

What's the difference between an elephant and
a strawberry?
*Strawberries are red.*

What's the difference between a sick elephant
and a dead bee?
*One's a seedy beast and the other's a bee
deceased.*

What's the difference between an elephant and
an egg?
*If you don't know that, I'm not trying one of
your omelettes!*

What's the difference between an elephant and
a sandwich?
*A sandwich doesn't weigh 2 tons.*

What's the difference between an elephant and a cherry?
*Have you ever tried eating elephant pie?*

What's the difference between an elephant and a large lettuce?
*One is a funny beast, the other is a bunny feast.*

What's the difference between a pickle and an elephant?
*A pickle always forgets.*

Why do pickles always forget?
*What do they have to remember?*

What's the difference between an elephant and snew?
*What's snew?*
Not a lot; what's new with you?

# Why . . .

Why wasn't the elephant allowed on the plane?
*Because his trunk wouldn't fit under the seat.*

Why couldn't the elephants play cards on the Ark?
*Because Noah was sitting on the deck.*

Why do elephants drink so much water?
*They don't like lemonade.*

Why aren't elephants white and shiny?
*Because if they were, they'd be fridges.*

Why do elephants have short tails?
*So they won't get stuck in revolving doors.*

Why did the elephant want to be alone?
*Because 2 is a crowd.*

Why are elephants so clever?
*They have lots of grey matter.*

**Why do elephants have trunks?**
*To go swimming.*

**Why else?**
*Because they don't have pockets.*

**Why else?**
*To put their tennis racquets in.*

**Why else?**
*Because they don't have glove compartments.*

**Why else?**
*Because bikinis don't suit them.*

**Why did the elephant book 2 seats on the coach?**
*So the person next to him wouldn't get squashed.*

**Why did the elephant cross the road?**
*Because he didn't want to listen to that last joke.*

**Why else?**
*Because the light was green.*

**Why else?**
*Because it was a trunk road.*

**Why else?**
*Because the subway was closed.*

**Why did the chicken cross the road?**
*Because it was tied to the elephant's leg.*

**Why are elephants slow to apologize?**
*It takes a long time for them to swallow their pride.*

Why shouldn't you tell an elephant joke while you are skating?
*The ice might crack up.*

Why shouldn't you grab an elephant by his tail?
*It may only be his tail, but it could be your end.*

Why was the elephant unhappy?
*Because he wasn't allowed to read* **Not the Elephant Joke Book.**

Why do elephants squirt water through their trunks?
*Because if they did it through their tails they'd find it difficult to aim straight.*

Why do elephants have grey hides?
*They'd look funny in tweed coats.*

Why does an elephant enjoy his food?
*He makes a little go a long way.*

Why did the elephant wear brown shoes?
*Because his black ones were at the cobbler's.*

Why do elephants float on their backs?
*So that they won't get their toes wet.*

Why did the elephant wear pink tennis shoes?
*Because white ones get so dirty.*

Why are elephants grey?
*So you can tell them apart from canaries.*

Why do elephants paint their toenails green, yellow, orange, red and black?
*So that they can hide in a bag of jelly babies.*

Why don't elephants have feathers?
*If they did, you would confuse them with ducks.*

What would happen if they did have?
*You'd be up to your armpits in feathers!*

Why do elephants live in zoos?
*They're cheaper than flats.*

Why are elephants poor dancers?
*Because they have 2 left feet.*

Why did the gardener put elephant manure on his garden?
*Because he wanted to grow trees with bigger trunks.*

Why do elephants have flat feet?
*They keep falling out of cherry trees.*

Why do elephants wear slippers?
*So they can sneak up on mice without being heard.*

Why do elephants wear woolly jumpers?
*If you bought* **The Woolly Jumper Joke Book**, *you'd know.*

Why didn't the elephant tip the bellboy when he checked into the hotel?
*Because he didn't carry the elephant's trunk up to his room.*

Why do elephants paint the soles of their feet brown?
*So that they can float upside down in the gravy.*

Why do elephants eat so many peanuts?
*Because people don't offer them anything else.*

**Why did the elephant scratch himself?**
*Because he was the only one who knew where the itch was.*


**Why are elephants safe from pickpockets?**
*Because they don't have pockets.*


**Why did the elephant go to the dentist?**
*Because he had a terrible tusk-ache.*

**Why did Adam call the elephant an 'elephant'?**
*Because it looked more like an elephant than anything else he'd seen.*

**Why do elephants eat leaves?**
*Because they can't cook.*

**Why don't elephants care what people say about them?**
*They're thick skinned.*

**Why don't elephants have dandruff?**
*Have you ever seen an elephant with long hair?*

**Why did the elephant lie in the middle of the road?**
*So it could trip up the cyclists.*

**Why else?**
*To trip up the chickens.*

Why is an elephant grey and hairy?
*Because if it was green and hairy it would be a
gooseberry.*

Why else?
*Because if it was brown and hairy it would be a
coconut.*

# How . . .

How do you stop an elephant from charging?
*Take away his credit cards.*

How do zoo animals greet each other?
*'Hi Ena!'; ''Ello Phant!'*

How do you know that peanuts are fattening?
*Have you ever seen a skinny elephant?*

How do you know if an elephant is visiting
your house?
*His bicycle will be parked outside.*

How do you make a banana laugh?
*Tell it an elephant joke.*

How do you get an elephant out of the bath?
*Pull the plug out.*

How do elephants have baths?
*They put their toes in first.*

How can an elephant best avoid wrinkling?
*He should avoid sleeping in his clothes.*

How do you make an elephant fly?
*Buy it an airline ticket.*

How did the elephant stop a cold going to his chest?
*He tied a knot in his trunk.*

How many elephants can you get in an empty cupboard?
*Only one; after that it isn't empty!*

When a 3-ton elephant fell down a 30-foot well, how did they get it out?
*Wet.*

How do you get an elephant through a small door?
*Unless he goes on a diet, you don't!*

How do you fit 5 elephants into a Citröen 2CV?
*2 in the front, 2 in the back, and the last one in the glove compartment.*

How do you catch an elephant?
*Take a fishing rod and put a peanut on the end.*

How can you tell if there's an elephant in your sandwich?
*It's too heavy to lift off the plate.*

How did ducks get flat feet?
*From trying to teach elephants to dance.*

How does an elephant overtake a tortoise?
*He steps on it!*

How do you make an elephant laugh?
*Tell it a banana joke.*

How can you raise baby elephants?
*With a crane.*

How do you shoot a purple elephant?
*With a purple elephant gun.*

63

How do you shoot a white elephant?
*Jump on his back, choke him till he's purple,*
*then shoot him with a purple elephant gun.*


How can you recognize an elephant?
*By the smell of peanuts on its breath.*


How can you tell when there's an elephant in
the custard?
*By the lumps.*


How do mammoths pass exams?
*With extinction.*


How do you catch an elephant?
*Make a noise like a peanut.*
Oh, you've heard this one before?
*No, but I've tried it, and it works.*

How do you make an elephant sit up and beg?
*Wave a peanut under its trunk.*


How do you hire an elephant?
*Put a brick under each foot.*

How do elephants travel?
*By ele-copter.*

How else?
*By jumbo jet.*

How do you get rid of an old elephant?
*Put it in a jumbo sale.*

How do you recognize elephants in a swimming
pool?
*They're the ones with the grey trunks.*

How did elephants get such long noses?
*By playing tug of war with crocodiles.*

How do you disguise an elephant?
*Give him a moustache and dark glasses.*

How do we know that peanuts are good for elephants' eyesight?
*Have you ever seen an elephant with glasses?*

# Who, Which, Where . . .

**Which elephants have the shortest legs?**
*The smallest ones.*

**Where do you find most elephants?**
*Between their heads and their feet.*

**Where do elephants cross the road?**
*Zebra squashings.*

**Where do elephants put their guests?**
*In the trunk room.*

**Which hotels do elephants like best?**
*Tusk House Forte hotels.*

**Who lost a herd of elephants?**
*Big Bo Peep.*

Where do elephants go for their holidays?
*Tuskany.*

If an African elephant fought an African tiger,
who'd win?
*Neither; there's no such thing as an African
tiger.*

If an elephant lost its tail, where would it get a
new one?
*The retailer's.*

If an elephant's trunk pointed north, where would its tail point?
*To the ground.*

Who is the better fighter, an elephant or a chicken?
*An elephant; he's no chicken.*

Who is the richest elephant in the world?
*Rockerfellerphant.*

Where should a 4-ton elephant go?
*On a diet.*

Who is the best tennis-playing elephant?
*Jumbo Connors.*

# Did you hear . . .

Did you hear about the elephant who went to the beach to see something new in trunks?

Did you hear about the man who saw a gardener pushing a wheelbarrow full of elephant manure? 'What are you going to do with that?', he asked. 'Put it on my gooseberries', the gardener said. 'Oh,' said the man, 'I usually put custard on mine.'

Did you hear about the man who got a job at the zoo cleaning out the elephant house? He's complaining that his work is piling up!

Did you hear the one about the 10-foot high elephant?
*Never mind, you'll never get over it.*

Did you hear the one about the elephant in a cherry tree?
*Never mind, it's way over your head.*

Did you hear the joke about the elephant who loved to juggle?
*Never mind, let's drop it.*

Did you hear about the elephant who went away to forget?

Did you hear about the elephant racing the other animals in the jungle? At the finishing post he was neck and neck with the lion, but he stuck out his trunk to win the race.

Did you hear about the man who walked into a pub with a baby elephant under his arm? 'Where on earth did you get that thing?' said the barman. 'I won him in a raffle,' said the elephant.

Did you hear about the elephant who walked into a pub and ordered a pint of beer? The barman charged him five pounds and said, 'We don't get many elephants in here.' 'I'm not surprised,' replied the elephant, 'the prices you charge!'

Did you hear about the man who took an elephant to the cinema? The manager expected it to go on the rampage, but it didn't. Afterwards he said to the man, 'I am really surprised; your elephant was very quiet and actually seemed to enjoy the film.' 'Yes,' said the man, 'I was surprised, too: he hadn't enjoyed the book.'

Did you hear about the elephant who went into a post office and said, 'Guess what I've just done?' The postmaster said, 'What?' And the elephant replied, 'Speak!'

# Jumbo talk . . .

CUSTOMER: I'd like an elephant sandwich.
WAITER: *I'm sorry sir, but elephant sandwiches are off.*
CUSTOMER: Why's that?
WAITER: *We've run out of bread.*

CUSTOMER: Waiter, there's a fly in my soup.
WAITER: *I'm sorry sir, you'll have to leave. This is an elephant joke book!*

CUSTOMER: Do you make life-size enlargements of photos?
CHEMIST: *Certainly, madam.*
CUSTOMER: Good, here's a photo of an elephant.

SCHOOLBOY: My sister's got a memory like an elephant.
FRIEND: *And a shape to match!*

SCHOOLBOY: I've got to write an essay on an elephant.
FRIEND: *Well, you'll need a ladder.*


CIRCUS VISITOR: How much do you sell elephants for?
TRAINER: *50 pence.*
VISITOR: That's cheap, 50 pence an elephant?
TRAINER: *No, 50 pence a pound.*


WALLY: I've decided to buy an elephant and keep it at home as a pet.
WALLY'S FRIEND: *What about the horrible smell?*
WALLY: The elephant will just have to get used to it.

WALLY: I've lost my pet elephant.
WALLY'S FRIEND: *Why not put an advert in the newspaper in the lost and found section?*
WALLY: What good would that be? My elephant can't read.

WALLY: I wish I had enough money to buy an elephant.
WALLY'S FRIEND: *What do you want with an elephant?*
WALLY: Nothing, I just wish I had that much money!

WALLY: I can shoot an elephant with one hand.
WALLY'S FRIEND: *Where did you see an elephant with one hand?*

# Jumbo jingles . . .

An elephant is big,
An elephant is fat,
It has no fingers,
It has no toes,
But goodness gracious
What a nose!

Hickory dickory dock,
The elephant ran up the clock,
The clock is being repaired . . .

# Tail-pieces . . .

Hannibal must have been the world's first genetic engineer; he crossed the Alps with elephants.

The definition of the impossible is an elephant hanging over a cliff with its tail round a daisy.

The definition of willpower is an elephant eating only one peanut.

The definition of an elephant is a mouse that's taken vitamin pills and been on a body-building course.

They say an elephant never forgets, but what has he got to remember?

When is an elephant most likely to enter your
house?
*When the door is open.*


When do elephants paint their toenails green?
*When they want to hide upside down in
gooseberry jam.*


Knock, knock.
*Who's there?*
Elephant.
*Elephant who?*
Elephantasizes about being a pop star.

Knock, knock.
*Who's there?*
Tusk.
*Tusk who?*
Tusk you to be nosey.


**Why did the elephant wear dark glasses?**
*With 2 Beaver joke books about him, he didn't want to be recognized.*